This book belongs to:

_____

_____

A Treasury for
One
Year Olds

A TREASURY FOR

One
Year Olds

*A Collection of Nursery Rhymes
and Lullabies*

p

Illustrated by Michelle White and Gaby Hansen
Designed by Jester Designs

This is a Parragon Publishing book
First published in 2003

Parragon Publishing
Queen Street House
4 Queen Street
Bath BA1 1HE, UK

ISBN 1-40540-021-8
Printed in China

✦ Contents ✦

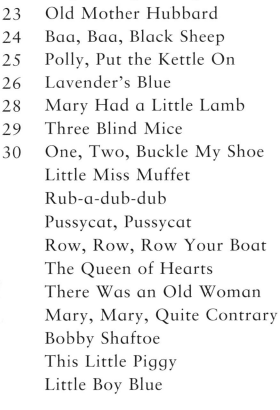

Nursery Rhymes

Bedtime Rhymes

Nursery Rhymes

Hey Diddle Diddle

Hey diddle diddle,
The cat and the fiddle,
The cow jumped over the moon;
The little dog laughed
To see such sport,
And the dish ran away with the spoon.

Here We Go 'Round the Mulberry Bush

Here we go 'round the mulberry bush,
The mulberry bush, the mulberry bush,
Here we go 'round the mulberry bush,
On a cold and frosty morning.

This is the way we wash our hands,
Wash our hands, wash our hands,
This is the way we wash our hands,
On a cold and frosty morning.

This is the way we brush our hair,
Brush our hair, brush our hair,
This is the way we brush our hair,
On a cold and frosty morning.

This is the way we go to school,
Go to school, go to school,
This is the way we go to school,
On a cold and frosty morning.

Pat-a-Cake

Pat-a-cake, pat-a-cake, baker's man,
Bake me a cake as fast as you can.
Roll it, and prick it, and mark it with a "B"
And put it in the oven for Baby and me!

The Grand Old Duke of York

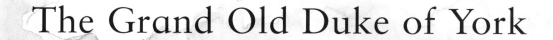

Oh, the grand old Duke of York,
He had ten thousand men,
He marched them up to the top of the hill,
And he marched them down again.

And when they were up they were up,
And when they were down they were down,
And when they were only half way up,
They were neither up nor down.

Ride a Cock Horse

Ride a cock horse to Banbury Cross
To see a fine lady upon a white horse.
Rings on her fingers and bells on her toes,
She shall have music wherever she goes.

Little Bo-Peep

Little Bo-Peep has lost her sheep,
And can't tell where to find them;
Leave them alone, and they'll come home,
And bring their tails behind them.

Jack and Jill

Jack and Jill went up the hill,
To fetch a pail of water;
Jack fell down, and broke his crown,
And Jill came tumbling after.

Then up Jack got, and home did trot,
  As fast as he could caper;
He went to bed, to mend his head,
  With vinegar and brown paper.

Little
Jack Horner

Little Jack Horner
Sat in the corner,
Eating his Christmas pie;
He put in his thumb,
And pulled out a plum,
And said, "What a good boy am I!"

Ring a-Round the Roses

Ring a-round the roses,
A pocket full of posies.
Ashes! Ashes!
We all fall down!

I Had a
Little Nut Tree

I had a little nut tree
And nothing would it bear.
But a silver nutmeg
And a golden pear.

The king of Spain's daughter
Came to visit me,
And all for the sake
Of my little nut tree.

Simple Simon

Simple Simon met a pieman
Going to the fair;
Said Simple Simon to the pieman,
"Let me taste your ware."

Mrs. Hen

Chook, chook, chook, chook, chook,
Good morning, Mrs. Hen.
How many chickens have you got?
Madam, I've got ten.
Four of them are yellow,
And four of them are brown.
And two of them are speckled red,
The nicest in the town.

Humpty Dumpty

Humpty Dumpty sat on a wall,
Humpty Dumpty had a great fall;
All the king's horses and all the king's men
Couldn't put Humpty together again.

Five Little
Monkeys

Five little monkeys
walked along the shore;
One went a-sailing,
Then there were four.

Four little monkeys
climbed up a tree;
One of them fell down,
Then there were three.

Three little monkeys
found a pot of glue;
One got stuck in it,
Then there were two.

Two little monkeys
found a raisin bun;
One ran away with it,
Then there was one.

One little monkey
cried all afternoon,
So they put him in an airplane
And sent him to the moon.

It's Raining,
It's Pouring

It's raining, it's pouring,
The old man is snoring;
He went to bed and bumped his head
And couldn't get up in the morning!

Hickory, Dickory, Dock

Hickory, dickory, dock. The mouse ran up the clock.
The clock struck one, the mouse ran down,
Hickory dickory, dock.

One, Two, Three, Four, Five

One, two, three, four, five,
Once I caught a fish alive.
Six, seven, eight, nine, ten,
Then I let it go again.
Why did you let it go?
Because it bit my finger so.
Which finger did it bite?
This little finger on the right.

Itsy Bitsy Spider

Itsy Bitsy spider,
Climbed up the water spout;
Down came the rain,
And washed the spider out;
Out came the sun,
And dried up all the rain;
So Itsy Bitsy Spider
Climbed up the spout again.

Sing a Song
of Sixpence

Sing a song of sixpence,
A pocket full of rye;
Four and twenty blackbirds
Baked in a pie.
When the pie was opened,
The birds began to sing;
Now, wasn't that a dainty dish
To set before the King?

32

The King was in his countinghouse,
Counting out his money;
The Queen was in the parlor
Eating bread and honey.
The maid was in the garden,
Hanging out the clothes.
Along there came a big blackbird
And snipped off her nose!

Old Mother Hubbard

Old Mother Hubbard
Went to the cupboard,
To fetch her poor dog a bone;
But when she got there
The cupboard was bare,
And so the poor dog had none.

Baa, Baa, Black Sheep

Baa, baa, black sheep,
Have you any wool?
Yes sir, yes sir,
Three bags full;
One for the master,
And one for the dame,
And one for the little boy
Who lives down the lane.

Polly, Put the Kettle On

Polly, put the kettle on,
Polly, put the kettle on,
Polly, put the kettle on,
We'll all have tea.
Sukey, take it off again,
Sukey, take it off again,
Sukey, take it off again,
They've all gone away.

Lavender's Blue

Lavender's blue, dilly, dilly,
Lavender's green;
When I am king, dilly, dilly,
You shall be queen.

Mary Had
a Little Lamb

Mary had a little lamb
Its fleece was white as snow;
And everywhere that Mary went
The lamb was sure to go.

It followed her to school one day,
Which was against the rules;
It made the children laugh and play
To see a lamb at school.

Three Blind Mice

Three blind mice, three blind mice.
See how they run, see how they run!
They all ran after the farmer's wife,
Who cut off their tails with a carving knife,
Did you ever see such a thing in your life,
As three blind mice.

One, Two, Buckle My Shoe

One, two,
Buckle my shoe;

Three, four,
Knock at the door;

Five, six,
Pick up sticks;

Seven, eight,
Lay them straight;

Nine, ten,
A good fat hen;

Eleven, twelve,
Dig and delve;

Thirteen, fourteen,
Maids a-courting;

Fifteen, sixteen,
Maids in the kitchen;

Seventeen, eighteen,
maids a-waiting;

Nineteen, twenty,
my plate's empty.

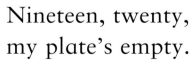

Little Miss Muffet

Little Miss Muffet
Sat on a tuffet,
Eating her curds and whey;
Along came a spider,
Who sat down beside her
And frightened Miss Muffet away.

Rub-a-dub-dub

Rub-a-dub-dub,
Three men in a tub,
And who do you think they be?
The butcher, the baker,
The candlestick-maker,
Turn them out, knaves all three.

Pussycat, Pussycat

Pussycat, pussycat, where have you been?
I've been to London to visit the Queen.
Pussycat, pussycat, what did you do there?
I frightened a little mouse under her chair.

Row, Row
Row your Boat

Row, row, row your boat
Gently down the stream.
Merrily, merrily, merrily, merrily,
Life is but a dream.

The Queen of Hearts

The Queen of Hearts,
She made some tarts
All on a summer's day.

The Knave of Hearts,
He stole the tarts
And took them clean away.

The King of Hearts,
Called for the tarts
And beat the Knave full sore.

The Knave of Hearts,
Bought back the tarts
And vowed he'd steal no more.

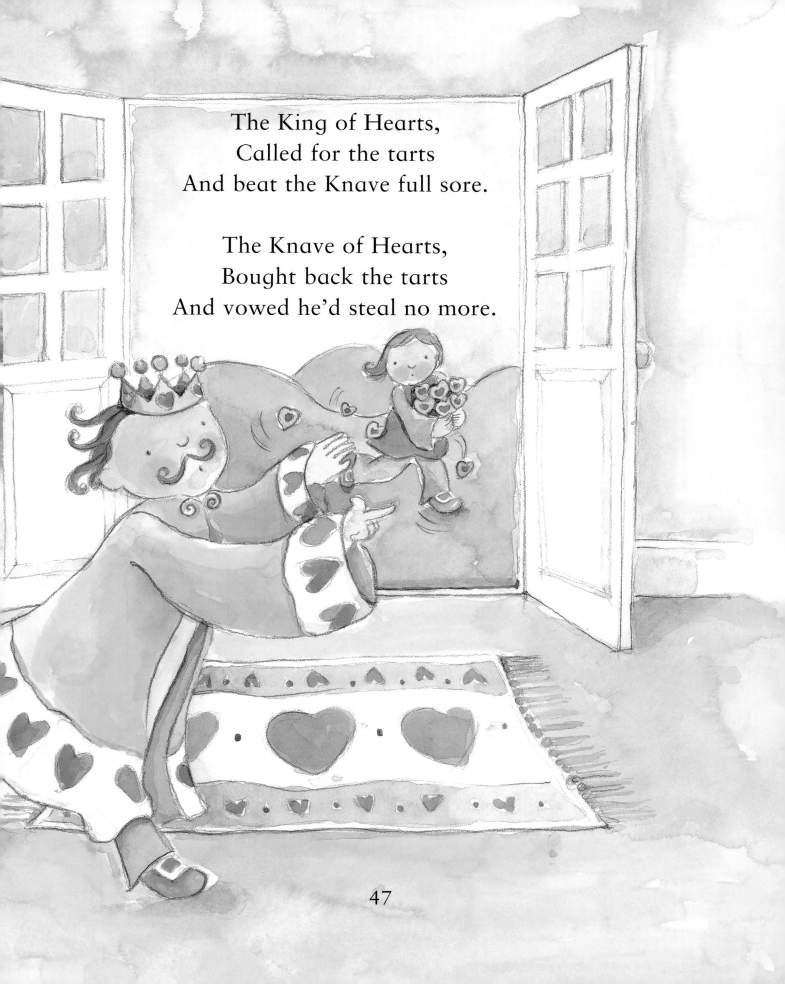

There was an Old Woman

There was an old woman
who lived in a shoe,
She had so many children
she didn't know what to do;
She gave them some broth
without any bread;
And scolded them soundly
and put them to bed.

Mary, Mary, Quite Contrary

Mary, Mary, quite contrary,
How does your garden grow?
With silver bells and cockle shells
And pretty maids all in a row.

Bobby Shaftoe

Bobby Shaftoe's gone to sea,
Silver buckles on his knee,
He'll come back and marry me,
Pretty Bobby Shaftoe.

This Little Piggy

This little
piggy went
to market,

This little
piggy stayed
at home,

This little
piggy had
roast beef,

And this
little piggy
had none,

And this little piggy cried
"Wee-wee-wee-we-wee"
All the way home.

Little Boy
Blue

Little Boy Blue, come blow your horn,
The sheep's in the meadow, the cow's in the corn.
Where is the boy that looks after the sheep?
He's under a haycock, fast asleep.
Will you wake him? No, not I!
For if I do, he's sure to cry.

Bedtime Rhymes

Golden Slumbers

Golden slumbers kiss your eyes,
Smiles await you when you rise;
Sleep, pretty baby, do not cry,
And I will sing a lullaby.

Thomas Dekker

Boys and Girls, Come Out to Play

Boys and girls, come out to play,
The moon doth shine as bright as day!
Leave your supper and leave your sleep,
And meet your playfellows in the street.
Come with a whoop and come with a call,
Come with a good will or not at all.

54

Up the ladder and down the wall,
A halfpenny loaf will serve us all.
You find milk, and I'll find flour,
And we'll have a pudding in half an hour.

55

I See the Moon

I see the moon,
And the moon sees me;
God bless the moon,
And God bless me.

56

Jack Be Nimble

Jack be nimble,
Jack be quick,
Jack jump over
The candlestick.

Up the
Wooden Hill

Up the wooden hill
to Bedfordshire.
Down Sheet Lane
to Blanket Fair.

Goosey, Goosey, Gander

Goosey, goosey, gander,
Whither shall I wander?
Upstairs and downstairs
And in my lady's chamber.
There I met an old man
Who would not say his prayers,
So I took him by the left leg
And threw him down the stairs.

Bed in Summer

In winter I get up at night
And dress by yellow candle-light.
In summer, quite the other way,
I have to go to bed by day.

I have to go to bed and see
The birds still hopping on the tree,
Or hear the grown-up people's feet
Still going past me in the street.

And does it not seem hard to you,
When all the sky is clear and blue,
And I should like so much to play,
To have to go to bed by day?

Robert Louis Stevenson

61

Little Fred

When little Fred went to bed,
He always said his prayers;
He kissed Mamma, and then Papa,
And straightway went upstairs.

Sleep Little Child

Sleep little child, go to sleep,
Mother is here by thy bed.
Sleep little child, go to sleep,
Rest on the pillow thy head.

The world is silent and still,
The moon shines bright on the hill,
Then creeps past the window sill.

Sleep little child, go to sleep,
Oh sleep, go to sleep.

Bedtime

The evening is coming, the sun sinks to rest;
The rooks are all flying straight home to the nest.
"Caw!" says the rook, as he flies overhead;
"It's time little people were going to bed!"

The flowers are closing; the daisy's asleep;
The primrose is buried in slumber so deep.
Shut up for the night is the pimpernel red;
It's time little people were going to bed!

64

The butterfly, drowsy, has folded its wing;
The bees are returning, no more the birds sing.
Their labor is over, their nestlings are fed;
It's time little people were going to bed!

Thomas Hood

Diddle, Diddle
Dumpling

Diddle, diddle, dumpling, my son John
Went to bed with his trousers on;
One shoe off, and the other shoe on,
Diddle, diddle, dumpling, my son John.

The Man
in the Moon

The man in the moon
came down too soon,
And asked his way to Norwich;
He went by the south,
and burnt his mouth
With supping cold pease-porridge.

Hush, Little Baby

Hush, little baby, don't say a word,
Papa's gonna buy you a mocking bird.

If that mocking bird don't sing,
Papa's gonna buy you a diamond ring.

If that diamond ring turns to brass,
Papa's gonna buy you a looking-glass.

If that looking-glass gets broke,
Papa's gonna buy you a billy goat.

If that billy goat don't pull,
Papa's gonna buy you a cart and mule.

If that cart and mule turn over,
Papa's gonna buy you a dog named Rover.

If that dog named Rover won't bark,
Papa's gonna buy you a horse and cart.

If that Horse and Cart fall down,
You'll still be the sweetest little baby in town.

Come to Bed,
says Sleepy-head

"Come to bed", says Sleepy-head
"Tarry a while," says Slow;
"Put on the pot,' says Greedy-gut,
"Let's sup before we go."

70

Bedtime

Down with the lambs
Up with the lark,
Run to bed children
Before it gets dark.

There Was an Old Woman Tossed Up in a Blanket

There was an old woman tossed up in a blanket,
Seventeen times as high as the moon;
But where she was going, no mortal could tell it,
For under her arm, she carried a broom.

"Old woman, old woman, old woman," said I,
"Whither, ah whither, ah whither so high?"
"To sweep the cobwebs from the sky."
"May I come with you?" "Aye, by and by."

Star Light,
Star Bright

Star light, star bright,
First star I see tonight,
I wish I may, I wish I might,
Have the wish I wish tonight.

Bye, Baby Bunting

Bye, baby bunting,
Daddy's gone a-hunting,
Gone to get a rabbit-skin,
To wrap my baby bunting in.

Teddy Bear, Teddy Bear

Teddy bear, Teddy bear,
Turn around.

Teddy bear, Teddy bear,
Touch the ground.

Teddy bear, Teddy bear,
Show your shoe.

Teddy bear, Teddy bear,
That will do.

Teddy bear, Teddy bear,
    Run upstairs.

Teddy bear, Teddy bear,
    Say your prayers.

Teddy bear, Teddy bear,
    Turn out the light.

Teddy bear, Teddy bear,
    Say goodnight.

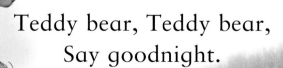

Rock-a-Bye, Baby

Rock-a-bye, baby, on the tree top;
When the wind blows, the cradle will rock;
When the bow breaks, the cradle will fall;
Down will come baby, cradle and all.

Wee Willie Winkie

Wee Willie Winkie
Runs through the town,
Upstairs and downstairs
In his nightgown.
Rapping at the window,
Crying through the lock,
Are the children all in bed?
It's past eight o'clock.

Go to Bed
First

Go to bed first,
A golden purse;

Go to bed second,
A golden pheasant;

Go to bed third,
A golden bird.

How Many Miles to Babylon?

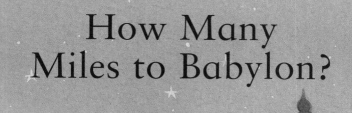

How many miles to Babylon?
Three score miles and ten.
Can I get there by candle-light?
Yes, and back again.
If your heels are nimble and light,
You may get there by candle-light.

Twinkle, Twinkle, Little Star

Twinkle, twinkle, little star,
How I wonder what you are!
Up above the world so high,
Like a diamond in the sky.

When the blazing sun is gone,
When he nothing shines upon,
Then you show your little light,
Twinkle, twinkle, all the night.

Then the traveler in the dark,
Thanks you for your tiny spark,
He could not see which way to go,
If you did not twinkle so.

In the dark blue sky you keep,
And often through my curtains peep,
For you never shut your eye,
'Til the sun is in the sky.

As your bright and tiny spark,
Lights the traveler in the dark—
Though I know not what you are,
Twinkle, twinkle, little star.

Jane Taylor

83

Go to Bed Late

Go to bed late,
Stay very small;
Go to bed early,
Grow very tall.

The Mouse's Lullaby

Oh, rock-a-bye, baby mouse, rock-a-bye, so!
When baby's asleep to the baker's I'll go,
And while he's not looking I'll pop from a hole,
And bring to my baby a fresh penny roll.

Palmer Cox

85

Sleep, Baby, Sleep

Sleep, baby, sleep,
Your father keeps the sheep;
Your mother shakes the dreamland tree
And from it fall sweet dreams for thee;
Sleep, baby, sleep.

Sleep, baby, sleep,
The large stars are the sheep;
The little stars are the lambs, I guess,
And the gentle moon is the shepherdess;
Sleep, baby, sleep.

Sleep, baby, sleep,
Your father keeps the sheep;
Your mother guards the lambs this night,
And keeps them safe till morning light;
Sleep, baby, sleep.

87

Tumbling

In jumping and tumbling
We spend the whole day,
'Til night by arriving
Has finished our play.

What then? One and all,
There's no more to be said,
As we tumbled all day,
So we tumble to bed.

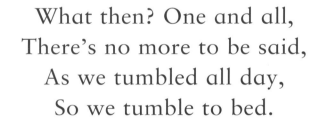

The Man in the Moon

The man in the moon looked out of the moon,
Looked out of the moon and said,
"'Tis time for all children on the earth
To think about getting to bed!"

89

Brahms' Lullaby

Lullaby, and good night,
With rosy bed light,
With lilies overspread,
Is my baby's sweet bed.

Lay you down now, and rest,
May your slumber be blessed!
Lay you down now, and rest,
May thy slumber be blessed!

Lullaby, and good night,
You're your mother's delight,
Shining angels beside
My darling abide.

Soft and warm is your bed,
Close your eyes and rest your head.
Soft and warm is your bed,
Close your eyes and rest your head.

Johannes Brahms

Now the Day is Over

Now the day is over,
Night is drawing nigh,
Shadows of the evening
Steal across the sky.

Now the darkness gathers,
Stars begin to peep,
Birds and beasts and flowers
Soon will be asleep.

Sabine Baring-Gould

92

Sleepy-Time

Sleepy-time has come for my baby,
Baby now is going to sleep.
Kiss Mama good night
And we'll turn out the light,
While I tuck you in bed
'Neath your covers tight.
Sleepy-time has come for my baby,
Baby now is going to sleep.

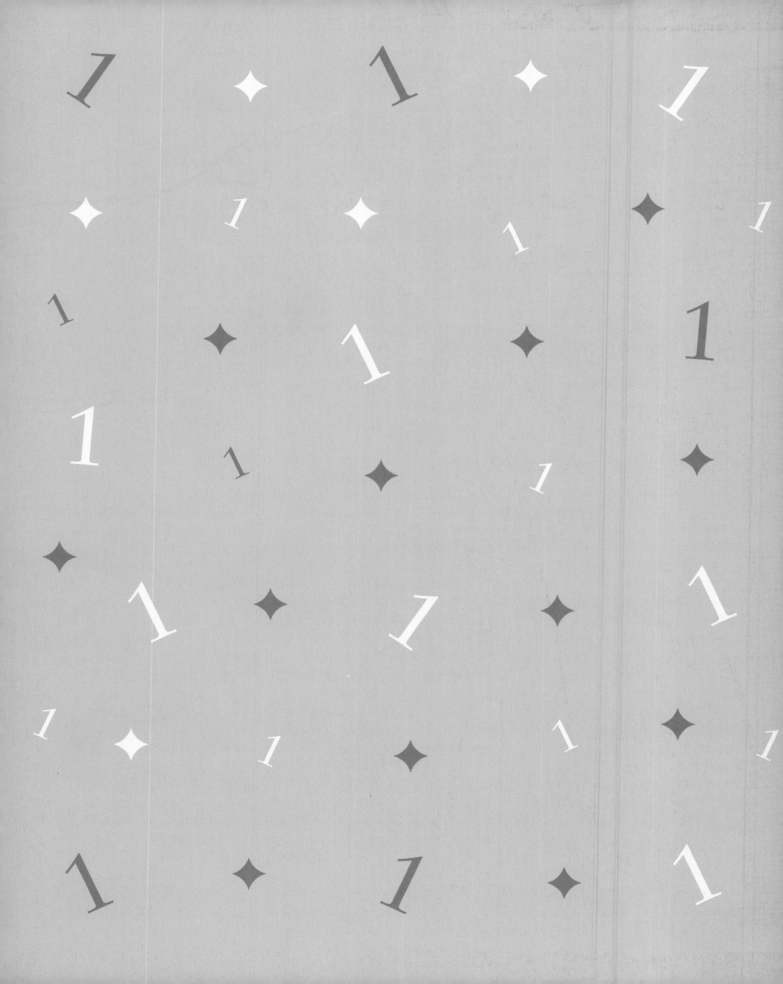